THROUGH T
WITH
WHO LET THE DADS OUT?

Published by
The Bible Reading Fellowship
15 The Chambers, Vineyard
Abingdon OX14 3FE
United Kingdom
Tel: +44 (0)1865 319700
Email: enquiries@brf.org.uk
Website: www.brf.org.uk
BRF is a Registered Charity

ISBN 978 1 84101 727 3

First published 2014
10 9 8 7 6 5 4 3 2 1 0

Acknowledgments
Unless otherwise stated, scripture quotations are taken from the Holy Bible, New International Version (Anglicised edition). Copyright © 1979, 1984, 2011 by Biblica. Used by permission of Hodder & Stoughton Publishers, an Hachette UK company. All rights reserved. 'NIV' is a registered trademark of Biblica. UK trademark number 1448790.

Cover photo: Luke Roberts

A catalogue record for this book is available from the British Library

Printed and bound by CPI Group (UK) Ltd, Croydon CR0 4YY

THROUGH THE YEAR WITH WHO LET THE DADS OUT?

A year's worth of ideas for reaching out to dads and their pre-school children

Mark Chester and Tony Sharp

For Dirk Uitterdijk—our friend and mentor and the original Hoole Baptist Church fatherhood pioneer. His influence permeates our work.

ACKNOWLEDGMENTS

Thanks to our families for allowing us to write about you and for your forbearance, especially when we have cocooned ourselves in the writing process and only managed grunts in response to your questions. We're back now.

Thanks to our friends throughout the Who Let The Dads Out? world and beyond. Your ideas, comments and stories inspire us.

Thanks to the Who Let The Dads Out? steering group for your enthusiasm and wisdom.

Thanks to our editor, Olivia Warburton, and the team at BRF for your leadership, guidance, patience and hard work.

We write to serve God, and our hope is that our words will play a part in giving his Holy Spirit a foothold in the hearts of men and their families.

CONTENTS

*

INTRODUCTION

Mark Chester

Things have changed a little since I wrote the first *Who Let The Dads Out?* book. Back then, I did not have my own laptop, so I borrowed my daughter Megan's, and consequently her online social life suffered for a considerable period of time. I wrote most of the book while sitting on our bed, because it was the only place I could find the peace and quiet I needed to concentrate. And, other than the craft ideas (which were my wife Su's handiwork), I could claim that all the words were my own.

This time around, I have my own laptop and I am writing at the dining-room table because Megan and Billy are not as distracting as they were when they were younger. In fact, it has been really helpful to run things past them and Su and pick their brains for ideas; and once again I have Su to thank for the craft ideas in the sections I have written. The biggest difference, though, is that I am now sharing the writing with a man who is as passionate about Who Let The Dads Out? and as committed to it as I am. His name is Tony Sharp, the Who Let The Dads Out? National Coordinator, and it is a great privilege to be co-authoring this book with him. It is also tremendous fun.

Tony brings with him a wealth of new thoughts and ideas and a perspective that is different from but complements my own. We hope that the combination of our voices engages and inspires you. Some have suggested that Tony and I are becoming a Who Let The Dads Out? double act and, of course, our thoughts turn immediately to the likes of Ant and Dec or Batman and Robin. Unfortunately, the people who say this to us are usually thinking about Laurel and Hardy or the Chuckle Brothers! We will let you make up your own minds about which is most accurate as you read through the pages of this book. We hope that we bring the proficiency of Torvill and Dean, the enthusiasm of Del Boy and Rodney, and the humour of Morecambe and Wise.

More seriously, as the number of Who Let The Dads Out? groups continues to grow, we want to equip and support you as you build relationships with the families in your communities and as you work to turn the hearts of fathers and children to one another and the hearts of all to their heavenly Father. Our sincere hope and prayer is that through this book, we can play a small part in helping 'to equip [God's] people for works of service, so that the body of Christ may be built up' (Ephesians 4:12).

*

HOW TO USE THIS BOOK

As Mark has indicated in his introduction, we have produced this book as a resource for the growing number of Who Let The Dads Out? groups that are being set up throughout the UK and overseas. We hope that this book will prove to be a useful resource for group leaders and helpers throughout the Who Let The Dads Out? year.

Before we go any further, we'd like to stress that when we talk about 'dads' we include all male carers and father figures—dads, stepdads, uncles, grandfathers, and so on. Whenever you see the word 'dad', please read it in this way.

The book outlines twelve monthly themed sessions. The themes might be linked to part of the church calendar or another celebration, or simply linked to the time of year. (Of course, there's no obligation to wait until January if you've purchased the book in June: just jump in at the most appropriate month!) Each of the themed sessions has two main components, as follows.

A reflection

Our reflections tie in with the themes for each month, relate to a verse or passage in the Bible (or, in one case, a hymn) and finish with a short prayer. The intention is that these reflections will help group leaders to prepare for the upcoming session.

When Mark started Who Let The Dads Out? it was all he and his team could do to buy the food and get to the church with enough time to set out the toys, start the coffee brewing and fire up the grill before the dads and children started arriving. But, setting aside our poor example, we'd like to challenge you to plan to get your volunteers together for ten minutes before the start of the session, to read through the reflection for the month and to spend a little while in prayer for the dads and children who come. We think this would be time really well spent.

An activity idea

You may already be an expert in coming up with brilliant and creative craft activities for young children to do with the help of an adult or teenager. If our ideas and guidance on craft activities appear pedantic, please bear in mind that we are men, and that our eyes glaze over whenever we enter Hobbycraft or a similar creative arts shop. Actually, you can go a long way without entering a craft shop. Remember, if the ideas we have included here appeal to you, chances are that they will appeal to the dads in your group. We recognise that dads will get stuck into a craft activity with their children if they're guided carefully along the way, but, to be on the safe side, we've tried to choose craft activities that are not too pink and fluffy. Some of the ideas have come from our wives, and, if you're a man and really struggling, we recommend that you appeal to the women in your life for help.

If some of the ideas we've included here don't work for you, just take the thematic idea and use it to target an internet search for other activity ideas. We know that it's good to have a germ of an idea to start from, so we hope our themes and activity ideas will act as that stimulus. The internet is jam-packed with ideas for craft activities for children, and we're grateful to all those who have the enthusiasm to share ideas through the worldwide web; without it, we would never have discovered and been able to bring you the delight that is Jericho toast!

What else have we included?

If you like an ordered life, then the structure of this book, in monthly themed sections, will probably tick your boxes. But maybe you're a bit more random in your approach; maybe you like to go off-piste or plough your own furrow. With this in mind, we have included a selection of other stories, case studies and ideas, sprinkled in between the monthly sections. A special acknowledgment must go to the wonderful people at Christian Vision for Men, who taught us that men love 'Top Ten' lists. Again, we hope that all these inserts will stimulate ideas that you can develop with your Who Let The Dads Out? group.

So there you have it. Congratulations, you've read the instruction manual before attempting to assemble the product (the most obvious thing in the world if you're a woman, but no small feat if you're a man), and you are ready to get stuck in.

Let's start with a job description.

*

WHAT DO YOU DO? A JOB DESCRIPTION FOR LEADERS

I ask lots of questions—sometimes too many—and when I am at a party it is never long before I enquire of somebody I have not met before, 'What do you do?' Recently, though, a friend of mine challenged me by saying that when he is in a social setting and meeting new people, he hates the question 'What do you do?' because he feels we should not be defined in that way. I could see his point, but was encouraged when he admitted that he still finds himself resorting to that very question when the conversation is drying up.

We set ourselves a mission to find an alternative question that could be just as effective in opening up a discussion with a new acquaintance but does not seem to define us by our work. I suspect we will not find a question that is as good at getting people to talk, because, let's face it, most of us are fairly comfortable chatting about how we spend our days.

We do seem to find it helpful to know and be able to express what we 'do' and why we are doing it, which is why most employment roles come with a job description. A written statement of purpose, responsibilities and skills helps us to know what we are working to achieve and how we will get there. A job description can give us comfort and structure, and means that we are always ready to answer the question 'What do you do?'

I have been thinking a lot about what we 'do' through Who Let The Dads Out? and have been trying to devise a job description. I thought it would be helpful to share some of these musings with you. A starting point for me has always been God's words expressed through the prophet Malachi: 'See, I will send you the prophet Elijah before that great and dreadful day of the Lord comes. He will turn the hearts of the fathers to their children, and the hearts of the children to their fathers; or else I will come and strike the land with a curse' (Malachi 4:5–6, NIV 1984).

In my book *Who Let The Dads Out?* I examined what these verses might mean and explored what impact God intended from the process of turning the hearts of fathers and children to one another. In recapping, it is worth considering that the words used in these verses are different depending on the translation of the Bible you read. Some refer to 'parents' and children and others to 'fathers' and children. The Hebrew means literally 'he will turn the hearts of fathers to sons and sons to their fathers.' Whichever way the words are translated, I believe that God's will for fathers and their children is clear. He wants their relationships to be strong because this will lead to the restoration of other family and community relationships. Fathers and children whose hearts have turned to one another help to establish peace and unity, and this leads to a model of strong families and strong communities, in which faith in God is passed from generation to generation.

About 420 years after Malachi's prophecy, God spoke again about turning the hearts of the fathers to their children—this time through the angel Gabriel. Gabriel appeared in the temple to the priest Zechariah to tell him that his prayers and those of his wife, Elizabeth, who were both 'well on in years', had been heard and that she would bear a son whose name would be John.

This is what Gabriel says about what John the Baptist will do: 'And he will go on before the Lord, in the spirit and power of Elijah, to turn the hearts of the fathers to their children and the disobedient to the wisdom of the righteous—to make ready a people prepared for the Lord' (Luke 1:17, NIV 1984).

We will return to examine the 'spirit and power of Elijah', but first I would like to focus on what John the Baptist is coming to do. Helpfully, it is summed up in just nine of Gabriel's words, and it is these nine words that, for me, define what we are doing through Who Let The Dads Out? These words identify our job purpose: 'to make ready a people prepared for the Lord'.

We are not running Who Let The Dads Out? groups just as Saturday morning social clubs for dads and their children. What we are doing is much more significant than that. Our job is 'to make ready a people prepared for the Lord'. In other words, we are leading people to Jesus—encouraging people to believe in and follow him—just as John the Baptist did. We must never lose sight of this purpose.

As we have already identified, one of the ways in which Gabriel says that John the Baptist will lead people to Jesus is by turning the hearts of the fathers to their children. Another way of looking at this is that it is one of our key duties, alongside turning the hearts of the children to their fathers, which contributes to achieving our job purpose. So we are beginning to build up a job description for what we do through Who Let The Dads Out? We know that our purpose is 'to make ready a people prepared for the Lord' and that our key duties are 'to turn the hearts of the fathers to their children and the hearts of the children to their fathers'.

Now we must identify the skills necessary for the job of a

Who Let The Dads Out? leader. To do that, we need to turn to the man who, according to Malachi's prophecy, God will send to turn hearts, and in whose spirit and power Gabriel says that John the Baptist will function—Elijah. I will attempt to define his 'spirit and power' by focusing on three of the characteristics I have observed in studying his life.

Patience

It is clear to me that Elijah was a patient man. The first time we encounter him in the Bible (1 Kings 17) is when he warns King Ahab about an impending drought. Just as Elijah has predicted, the rains stop. At this point, Elijah must think he has made it. He has secured the ear of the king and his forecast has proved to be spot-on. He could reasonably expect to become a regular and respected royal adviser. Certainly, if I had participated in such a successful audience with a monarch, I would be looking forward to great things. But God tells Elijah to retreat, and his exile lasts for three and a half years before God tells him to return to the king. Elijah spends part of this period alone in a ravine, being fed by ravens, and for the remaining time he lives with a widow and her son. It is a lengthy period of obscurity and waiting.

Our perception of how God works is often that he will spend a short period preparing us for a long ministry, whereas God's pattern can be that he spends a long time preparing us for a relatively short ministry. Development of any ministry (a Who Let The Dads Out? ministry included) can involve periods of waiting and times when we must be patient. Perhaps you would like to start a group but you do not have any volunteers to run it with you. Maybe your church leaders are not as keen on the idea as you are. You may have started a group already but are struggling to get dads to come along, or you may have a thriving group but do not feel that anybody is getting any closer to making a commitment to following Jesus. Our expectations and God's timing do not always coincide, so sometimes we just have to be patient and wait. This does not mean that we do nothing or give up; we must always make sure we are prepared to respond when needed. However, some patches of soil require short bursts of preparatory work and longer periods of waiting before they are ready to sustain growth. Perhaps you are in a preparatory period with your Who Let The Dads Out? group, but please do recognise that, if the soil is tended properly at this time, you are giving the ministry its best chance to bloom in the future.

Listening

There is a beautiful account of Elijah listening to God on Mount Horeb (1 Kings 19:11–12), which never fails to move me.

The Lord said, 'Go out and stand on the mountain in the presence of the Lord, for the Lord is about to pass by.' Then a great and powerful wind tore the mountains apart and shattered the rocks before the Lord, but the Lord was not in the wind. After the wind there was an earthquake, but the Lord was not in the earthquake. After the earthquake came a fire, but the Lord was not in the fire. And after the fire came a gentle whisper.

God spoke to Elijah by gently whispering his plans for what he wanted Elijah to do next—which was to anoint two future kings and call Elisha as his successor. I love the image of being spoken to in a gentle whisper, and I feel that it is more akin to the way God communicates with me. I have rarely, if ever, heard God shout his messages to me. Rather, his promptings to me have come more subtly, through words in the Bible that I have been guided to by others, scenes in films, small acts of loving kindness that I have had the privilege to observe, comments friends have made, stories in books, photographs, art and architecture, and through just being given space to think. The thing about a gentle whisper is that it is more difficult to hear than a loud shout and requires a greater degree of effort on the part of the listener. We must listen intentionally and persistently to avoid missing God's gentle whispers.

At the beginning of a new relationship, listening is often quite easy. When I met my wife, Su, I desperately wanted to listen to her, but now that we have been married for over 20 years I have to admit that things are a little different. I have to work harder to listen to her. If you have been a Christian for some time, perhaps listening to God is more difficult than when you first began to follow Jesus, and maybe you allow yourself to become distracted more easily; I know I do. I've found it helpful to try to understand what distracts me most from listening to God. For example, I have realised that when I find myself with job security and, consequently, financial security, I rely on God less. I stop listening and I miss his gentle whispers.

In establishing and developing your Who Let The Dads Out? ministry, I would encourage you to listen hard for the gentle whispers of God. You may find he is prompting you to ask someone to be a co-leader, or he could be nudging you to draw alongside a particular family in your group. Whatever it is that God whispers in your ear, please do respond. This leads us to the third aspect of Elijah's spirit and power that I would like us to consider.

Obedience

Throughout Elijah's life, God speaks and Elijah obeys. For example, 'Then the word of the Lord came to him: "Go at once to Zarephath in the region of Sidon and stay there. I have instructed a widow there to supply you with food." So he went to Zarephath' (1 Kings 17:8–10); and 'The word of the Lord came to Elijah: "Go and present yourself to Ahab, and I will send rain on the land." So Elijah went to present himself to Ahab' (18:1–2). And so it goes on, all the way through Elijah's story. God speaks and Elijah obeys. Even when God tells Elijah to go to King Ahaziah, Ahab's son, to tell him that he will die, Elijah dutifully does as he is instructed. It says in 2 Kings 1:4, 'So Elijah went.'

It is worth noting, however, that Elijah obeyed God one step at a time. He did not want to know everything that would happen in the future; he did not seek to understand where God was leading him before he would commit himself to doing what God told him. He listened, heard God speak, and obeyed.

To be honest, this approach to life makes me feel pretty uncomfortable. I like to anticipate how things will turn out and make plans—and also develop a back-up plan as a safety net. I like to feel secure and in control. But when I look back at my life, the times when God has most blessed my work have been when I have just taken the next step and trusted him for the rest. The development of the Who Let The Dads Out? movement is a good example. We began it in 2003 as a one-off session at our church, Hoole Baptist Church in Chester. We did not have a master plan to turn it into a national and international movement, or a strategy for how we would lead the men we were working with to explore their faith. We simply prayed and took what seemed to be the next logical step. Some things worked and others did not, but when we looked back we could clearly see God's plan in all that we had done.

I would like to encourage you to leave things in God's hands. God provided for Elijah one day at a time. In fact, after Elijah's first audience with King Ahab, God led him to the Kerith ravine and fed him quite literally one day at a time. Ravens brought Elijah bread and meat in the morning and again each evening. I guess he would have been, at times, extremely anxious about whether the birds would turn up or not, and what they would bring (I know I would have been) but he trusted God, and God fed him.

In developing a Who Let The Dads Out? ministry, I suggest that you do not get too far ahead of yourself. I know this is a pretty countercultural piece of advice, but I would recommend that you avoid the temptation to over-strategise. Concentrate your efforts on trying to discern what God wants you to do next, and then obey. Leave the master plan to the master.

To summarise, we have now built up a Bible-based job description for a Who Let The Dads Out? leader, which looks like this:

Purpose
- To make ready a people prepared for the Lord

Responsibilities
- To turn the hearts of the fathers to their children
- To turn the hearts of the children to their fathers

Skills
- Patience
- Good listening
- Obedience

For those who are already Who Let The Dads Out? leaders, I hope the process of answering the question 'What do you do?' has been helpful in clarifying your calling from God to fatherhood ministry. For those who are just exploring Who Let The Dads Out?, I hope these thoughts will give you a better understanding of why this is a ministry inspired by God.

I want to see more and more churches reaching out to the fathers and children in their communities because I believe that as the Who Let The Dads Out? movement grows, we will see a nation-changing effect. Families will be strengthened, communities will be invigorated, and men and their families will put their trust in God and pass that faith on to the next generation. It is clear to me that God intends to use the restoration of the relationships between fathers and children to lead people to him, so be encouraged that through your Who Let The Dads Out? ministry you are doing God's work.

There it is, the ultimate answer to the question 'What do you do?': 'I do God's work.'

*

— JANUARY —

IT'S NOT ROCKET SCIENCE

To borrow a concept from a famous song in a very famous film, we want to start at the very beginning because it's a very good place to start—but the beginning for Who Let The Dads Out? is not do-re-mi; rather, it is turning hearts. With Valentine's Day falling next month, we will be focusing on hearts again, so rather than having two heart-themed crafts in succession, we have chosen a winter craft this month and saved hearts for the month of romance!

January reflection

See, I will send you the prophet Elijah before that great and dreadful day of the Lord comes. He will turn the hearts of the fathers to their children, and the hearts of the children to their fathers; or else I will come and strike the land with a curse.
MALACHI 4:5–6 (NIV 1984)

When describing Who Let The Dads Out? I have often found myself using that old cliché, 'It's not rocket science' and, let's face it, it's not. Essentially it is about opening up the church, putting out toys, making tea, coffee and bacon butties and welcoming everyone in. It is what many of our churches have been doing for years in one way or another.

I would go as far as to say that it is what we are best at. But please do not misunderstand me; I am not dismissing what we do, or taking it lightly. I believe that Who Let The Dads Out? is incredibly powerful, but we do have to admit that we are not in the rocket science business.

So what business are we in? I believe that we are in the business of turning hearts. Hearts are incredible pieces of equipment. They can be open or closed, soft or hard, kind or cruel. Hearts can be 'in' some things but not in others, and hearts can melt, be stolen and break. Hearts can also be turned, and Who Let The Dads Out? is a place in which God can make this happen.

The prescription for turning a heart is, very simply, 'time'. Look around your Who Let The Dads Out? group this month and watch what is happening when a father and his children spend time together. You may notice one father feeding his son; another may be protecting his daughter from hurting herself on the slide, and a grandfather and child could be reading a story together. Children will be showing their fathers what to do with some of the toys and proudly showing off what they have made at the craft table. Fathers will be comforting, disciplining and cuddling their children. I am pretty certain that everywhere you look, you will see evidence of hearts turning and relationships deepening.

Perhaps, then, after all I have said, what we do at Who Let The Dads Out? *is* as complicated as rocket science and, arguably, more important. You see, I have come to the conclusion that we are in the business of heart surgery.

Thank God for each of the families at your Who Let The Dads Out? group and pray that their hearts will turn to one another. Ask that their hearts will also be turned to God, their Father in heaven, and pray for opportunities to help this process happen.

Father God, thank you for all of the fathers and children who walk through the doors of our church for Who Let The Dads Out? Please don't allow any to walk out again without their hearts having turned to one another. Please give us opportunities to show your love for these families and open their hearts in readiness to receive it. Amen

January activity: Snow biscuits

You will need:
- Rich Tea biscuits
- White icing sugar
- White mini marshmallows
- Edible glitter sprinkles (optional)
- Paper plates
- Teaspoons
- Clear sandwich bags (large enough to contain the paper plates)

Preparation

Make a bowl of white icing by following the instructions on the box of icing sugar.

Make sure the children have washed their hands.

The families must:

- Take a paper plate and two or three biscuits.
- Use a teaspoon to drizzle icing over each biscuit.
- Use the back of the teaspoon to smooth the icing over the whole surface of the biscuit, turning it into a snowy landscape.
- Quickly add snowdrifts by scattering mini-marshmallows over the wet icing.
- Add a dusting of edible glitter to give the snow its sparkle.
- Write the child's name on the paper plate and put it to one side to allow the icing to dry.
- At the end of the session, put the paper plate, with the snow biscuits on it, into a sandwich bag so that the treats will survive the journey home.

The craft leader must:

- Taste at least one completed snow biscuit with a lovely cup of tea.

The children may be desperate to eat their snow biscuits, so, with their fathers' permission, you could encourage them to prepare one biscuit to eat at Who Let The Dads Out? and the others to take home—ensuring they have prepared enough for every member of the family to have one each. You could suggest that the whole family eats their biscuits together.

*

GOD SLOT, OR NOT?

One of the challenges we often receive when talking about Who Let The Dads Out? to churches is 'Where do you talk about God during your sessions?' Some people feel that if there isn't a 'God slot', then Who Let The Dads Out? is no more than a social exercise.

I hear what these people are saying, and I invariably offer a number of mollifications, such as:

- 'We are not prescriptive: if your group feels it is right to build a short talk in—around a storytime, for example—then go for it.'
- 'For the most part, we see the evangelistic opportunity in a Who Let The Dads Out? session to be in the conversations that you (as leaders) will have with the dads who come, as you start to journey together.'
- 'We see Who Let The Dads Out? as a gateway ministry, that will allow you to build community with these dads and go on a journey together where more evangelistic opportunities will exist.'

All this is true, and I'll happily repeat it to anyone who doesn't quite get what we're trying to do with Who Let The Dads Out? But today I was both challenged and encouraged by an article by Jay Pathak in New Wine's quarterly magazine. The article was entitled 'Who is my neighbour?' and in it Jay explained how, as a group of church leaders in his city in the USA, he and others were challenged as individuals to seek out and meet their immediate neighbours. At the end of the article, Jay made a simple, possibly controversial but, I believe, quite liberating statement: 'We should love our neighbours because we are converted, not to convert them.'

I would stress that the article also gives due recognition to Jesus' great commandment in Matthew 22:39, so I'm confident that Jay wants his neighbours to know Jesus. But we shouldn't see our neighbours as a project. If we do, there is a danger that (a) it will be about us, not them, and (b) we will give up on them. Just as we'd never stop loving our children if they didn't become Christians, so we are challenged to start loving and keep on loving our neighbours.

What does this mean for your Who Let the Dads Out? group? I think it might mean the following:

- The primary purpose should be to create an opportunity to meet with men in your community—your neighbours. It's enough that you are creating the opportunity to get to know these guys. We believe that Who Let The Dads Out? has a positive spiritual impact on society, regardless of whether dads are responding to God.
- You shouldn't let the organisation and administration of the group become an end in itself. This is substituting busyness for being a good neighbour, and is a common error that we can all fall into.
- Strategically, it's important to take a long-term view. Think about how you will keep a sense of community going among the dads who currently attend, as their kids get older and they move out of the group. Equally, there will always be a supply of young dads in your neighbourhood, so your Who Let The Dads Out? group should, in principle, be unending. Have a mind towards succession

management, finding future potential group leaders, who might well be young dads themselves.
- Numbers are not the be-all and end-all. A small group means that you can develop closer relationships with individual dads.

Above all, I want you to be encouraged. Whenever I read about how the church is engaging with local communities through community-focused initiatives, activities and enterprises, such as Redeeming Our Communities, Christians Against Poverty, foodbanks, Caring for Ex-Offenders and, yes, Who Let The Dads Out?, I am reminded that the church is the hope of the nation. Let's believe it!

*

— FEBRUARY —

THE MOST EXCELLENT WAY

It's February and, for many men, our thoughts are obliged to turn towards the tricky issue of Valentine's Day and finding fresh ways to express how much we love our wives/partners/girlfriends with cards and possibly gifts.

In January Mark reflected on how Who Let The Dads Out? helps to turn the hearts of fathers to their children and the hearts of children to their fathers. This month we're going to dig a bit deeper into the love we feel as parents towards our children.

February reflection

And yet I will show you the most excellent way.

If I speak in the tongues of men or of angels, but do not have love, I am only a resounding gong or a clanging cymbal. If I have the gift of prophecy and can fathom all mysteries and all knowledge, and if I have a faith that can move mountains, but do not have love, I am nothing. If I give all I possess to the poor and give over my body to hardship that I may boast, but do not have love, I gain nothing.

Love is patient, love is kind. It does not envy, it does not boast, it is not proud. It does not dishonour others, it is not self-seeking, it is not easily angered, it keeps no record of wrongs. Love does not delight in evil but rejoices with the truth. It always protects, always trusts, always hopes, always perseveres.

Love never fails. But where there are prophecies, they will cease; where there are tongues, they will be stilled; where there is knowledge, it will pass away. For we know in part and we prophesy in part, but when completeness comes, what is in part disappears. When I was a child, I talked like a child, I thought like a child, I reasoned like a child. When I became a man, I put the ways of childhood behind me. For now we see only a reflection as in a mirror; then we shall see face to face. Now I know in part; then I shall know fully, even as I am fully known.

And now these three remain: faith, hope and love. But the greatest of these is love.

1 CORINTHIANS 12:31—13:13

Back in 2000, Universal Pictures released a film based on the Dr Seuss book *How the Grinch Stole Christmas*, with Jim Carrey in the title role. With a five-year-old daughter, it was a no-brainer that we were off to the cinema to see this one. The basic storyline is that the Grinch has lost the capacity to love. As he becomes more isolated and self-absorbed, his heart shrivels and his misery becomes self-perpetuating. Of course there is a happy ending: a young girl awakens compassion in our hairy green friend, his heart begins to swell once more and he is embraced again by the community that he has terrorised.

It may be a bit twee, but there is a lot of wisdom in this storyline. Metaphorically we are all born with 'open hearts' and we have a huge capacity to love, but the hardships of this world can mean that we lose that capacity. Even as Christians, we are not immune. Though our hearts may have burst open again as we recognised what Jesus did for us, repented and embraced God as our spiritual father, remember what John says to the church of Ephesus in Revelation 2:4: 'Yet I hold this against you: you have forsaken the love you had at first.'

I see our life's journey as a challenge and opportunity to grow more 'open-hearted' towards everyone—not just those dear to us, but even those who have hurt us or whom we see hurting others. God knows it's a difficult challenge, but as we bring this challenge to God, asking for his help, he does pour out his grace and our hearts will swell again.

I'd encourage you to reflect on the dads and male carers in your group. Some may be easier to get along with than others, but they all attend because they are trying to be good parents to their children. You can probably conjure positive (and sometimes negative) images of each of them as they interact with their children. Use these images to help you open your heart in love towards the men in your group, and then pray for each of them.

Father God, we are reminded that love is patient and love is kind. It does not envy, it does not boast, it is not proud. It does not dishonour others, it is not self-seeking, it is not easily angered, it keeps no record of wrongs. Love does not delight in evil but rejoices with the truth. It always protects, always trusts, always hopes, always perseveres. We pray that you will fill our hearts with love for the men in our group and that you will fill the hearts of each of the men with this love for the children in their care. Amen

February activity: Heart pendants

You will need:

- Pre-cut paper strips, ideally in lots of different colours
- Decorating materials. Choose one or more options: (Option 1) coloured felt-tip pens; (Option 2) tubes of glitter and PVA glue; (Option 3) flat-backed plastic coloured jewels and PVA glue
- Ribbon
- Scissors
- A stapler

Preparation

This activity is simple to prepare and simple to do. You'll need to cut some coloured paper strips, decide which decorating method you want the craft to involve, and prepare one or more examples. If you have access to a paper cutter, the preparation will be much easier than if you are using scissors.

The heart pendant uses three strips of different lengths, to create hearts within hearts. Simply cut three strips of about 20 mm width, at lengths of approximately 29 cm (a sheet of A4), 24 cm and 19 cm. You can use any colours, and it's probably best to generate a mixture so that the children can choose the colours they want.

The decoration is the main part of the activity that the children will be able to do, so it's important to give this some thought. In all cases they will decorate the longest of the three bits of paper, as this strip forms the outside of the heart. For decorating options 1 and 2, it would be best to decorate before making the pendant. For option 3, it is easier to add the decoration after making.

Prepare example(s) as follows (see the illustration on page 104).

Take the three strips of paper and fold each one in half. Open them out and lay them together at their creases, with the longest strip on top of the middle-length one, on top of the shortest one. Fold them up again, all together, and tuck the two ends of a loop of ribbon in at the centre of the fold. Staple just up from the fold, trapping the two ends of ribbon inside all three strips of paper. Now turn the paper strips back on themselves to form heart shapes, bringing all the ends together at the same point. This will create three hearts of different sizes within each other. Staple the ends all together and the heart pendant is complete.

The families must:

- Have fun together decorating one or more pendants.
- For option 1, draw and write a message on the longest strip of paper (making sure it is on the face matching the inside of the fold, as this will form the outside of the pendant). For example, they could write 'I love Daddy' or 'I love Mummy' or both. They could make a pendant for grandparents, schoolteachers, friends, and so on.
- For option 2, put PVA glue on the longest strip (make sure it is on the face matching the inside of the fold, as this will form the outside of the pendant), and then sprinkle glitter on to the glue.
- For option 3, put some dabs of PVA glue on the outside of the finished pendant, and then stick plastic jewels on to it.

Dad must feel a sense of having achieved 'crafting grade II' by emerging from this activity having successfully constructed a three-dimensional shape from three strips of paper, without having put a staple through his finger.

The craft leader must:

- Show and tell, helping the dads and children along.
- Encourage the dads and children to make several hearts, as they are simple to do.
- Not mind getting covered in glitter.

*

— MARCH —

I LOVE YOU, MUM

Here in the UK, March is when we celebrate Mothering Sunday, or Mother's Day. Given the emphasis in Who Let The Dads Out? on strengthening families, it certainly feels appropriate to encourage groups, dads and children to give thanks for and celebrate mums, so this is our theme for the month.

We recognise that some of the dads in your group may no longer be with the mother of some or all of the children they bring to Who Let The Dads Out? If the relationship remains amicable, the idea of preparing gifts for Mum won't be an issue, but in some cases the relationship may be difficult or may not exist at all. Needless to say, you should be mindful of the needs of your group of dads, and tailor the activities and session accordingly.

March reflection

But the angel said to her, 'Do not be afraid, Mary, you have found favour with God. You will conceive and give birth to a son, and you are to call him Jesus. He will be great and will be called the Son of the Most High. The Lord God will give him the throne of his father David, and he will reign over Jacob's descendants forever; his kingdom will never end.'

'How will this be,' Mary asked the angel, 'since I am a virgin?'

The angel answered, 'The Holy Spirit will come on you, and the power of the Most High will overshadow you. So the holy one to be born will be called the Son of God. Even Elizabeth your relative is going to have a child in her old age, and she who was said to be unable to conceive is in her sixth month. For no word from God will ever fail.'

'I am the Lord's servant,' Mary answered. 'May your word to me be fulfilled.' Then the angel left her.

LUKE 1:30–38

It was in March 2003 that the first Who Let The Dads Out? session took place, on the Saturday morning preceding Mothering Sunday. The session was promoted through the church parent-and-toddler group as a chance for mums to have a morning off. On the day, 20 dads turned up with assorted babies and toddlers, many of them delivered to the church by their wives and partners, who were determined to have a couple of child-free hours.

Mothering Sunday was certainly a good hook on which to hang that first session, and it seems appropriate, if the timing is right, to plan your March Who Let The Dads Out? session on the theme of mothers.

The Christian tradition of Mothering Sunday dates back to at least the 16th century, when servants were given the day off to visit their mother church. Only the connection with Mother's Day, which started in the USA in the early 20th century, gives us the mother-centric event that we celebrate today.

An American called Anna Jarvis successfully campaigned for a national Mother's Day in the USA, after the death of her own mother, and it was Constance Penswick-Smith who helped to re-establish the Mothering Sunday tradition in the UK by linking it to Anna's ideas of thanksgiving for our mothers. Anna herself quickly became dismayed by the growing commercialisation of the day, even disapproving of pre-printed Mother's Day cards. 'A printed card means nothing,' she said, 'except that you are too lazy to write to the woman who has done more for you than anyone in the world.'

We've chosen the verses above, from Luke 1, because they remind us of the servant-heart of Mary and of mothers everywhere. There is something undoubtedly stoical and heroic about bringing a child into this world, which we men need to respect fully. Often we baulk at the sacrifices we are asked to make when we become parents, but the reality is they are normally small compared to those made by our children's mothers.

For Mary, the sacrifice she was being asked to make was even bigger. An unplanned pregnancy, potential disgrace and the breakdown of her engagement to Joseph were what she might have expected to face immediately, and in later life it became clear that even more was being asked of her. Yet she didn't argue against God but humbly accepted his will.

In her way, my own mother has dedicated her life to the men around her (my dad, my brother and me), and I often thank God for what she has done for me. You may have similar feelings towards your own mother. So let's use this session to help the children appreciate their mums and create their own gifts and thank-you cards. Maybe it will glorify God in the heavens and bring a smile to the faces of Mary and Anna Jarvis too.

Dear Lord, this month we are reminded that mums are amazing. They are gentle, loving and kind. We often think of you as a Father God, but it is good also to recognise that there is so much goodness demonstrated through a mother's love for her child. We pray for our own mothers, the mothers of our children and of the children in our group. May they be blessed by the gifts taken home from this Who Let The Dads Out? session, way beyond the physical nature of the gift itself. Amen

March activity: Cupcake gifts

You will need:

- Alternative 1: the ingredients to make cupcakes (see below)
- Alternative 2: cupcake mix packs, available from all supermarkets
- Alternative 3: pre-baked plain cupcakes, available from all supermarkets
- Box of white icing sugar
- Edible decorations
- Gift box template (see page 105)
- A4 card
- PVA glue
- Ribbon

Cupcake recipe (makes 24)

- 170 g (6 oz) butter or margarine
- 170 g (6 oz) sugar
- 3 eggs
- 170 g (6 oz) self-raising flour
- 24 paper cake cases

Method

1. Preheat the oven to 180°C/Gas Mark 4.
2. Line a muffin tin with paper cases.
3. Mix the margarine and sugar together until light and fluffy. Add eggs one at a time, beating continuously. Sift in flour and mix gently.
4. Spoon the mixture into the paper cases.
5. Bake for 20 minutes until golden brown.
6. Stand to cool on a wire rack.

Preparation

Unless you are buying pre-baked cupcakes, you will need to bake them before the session. Be sure to make plenty: we think they'll be popular.

Photocopy the template of the gift box on to the A4 card (enough for one per family).

On the day, mix up a bowl of icing, following the instructions on the box.

If you're feeling particularly adventurous, why not colour your icing or even use fondant icing for that professional cupcake look? Too much? Yeah, I thought so too.

The families must:

- Decorate one or more cupcakes with icing and decorations, ensuring that they leave one for Mum.
- Colour in the gift box and then assemble it by folding and gluing the tabs. Leave the box to dry before inserting Mum's cupcake.
- Tie the box closed with a ribbon.

The craft leader must:

- Lick out the icing bowl at the end?

*

TOP TEN CARTOON CHARACTERS

Here's an activity to get the dads talking during your session. If your sessions include school-age children, they can get involved, too.

Ask them to make a list of the ten best cartoon characters of all time, counting down to number one.

You can create your own list in advance and compare lists towards the end of the session. Alternatively, you can use our list:

1. Dangermouse
2. Popeye
3. Super Mario
4. Jessica Rabbit
5. Scooby Doo
6. Mickey Mouse
7. Fred Flintstone
8. Papa Smurf
9. SpongeBob SquarePants
10. Homer Simpson—Doh!

*

— APRIL —

HE IS RISEN

Easter is an obvious opportunity to bring a gospel focus to your planning, and we'd really encourage you to incorporate some Easter theming into your activities, if you think this is appropriate and would work. Alternatively, think about using the Easter period to put on a social event that will allow some simple conversations to develop around the Easter story.

April reflection

Were you there when they crucified my Lord?
Were you there when they crucified my Lord?
Oh! Sometimes it causes me to tremble, tremble, tremble;
Were you there when they crucified my Lord?

Were you there when they nailed him to the tree? …

Were you there when they laid him in the tomb? …

Were you there when God raised him from the dead?
Were you there when God raised him from the dead?
Oh! Sometimes I feel like shouting glory! glory! glory!
Were you there when God raised him from the dead?
TRADITIONAL AMERICAN FOLK HYMN

As I contemplated a suitable Easter Bible passage for this section, I found myself drawn towards quoting the words of a hymn instead, so I hope you'll indulge me just this once.

I love a good hymn, and you can't go too far wrong with an American spiritual like this one. I love the slow burn of this hymn—the quiet, brooding sadness of the first three verses, followed by the great shout of joy that follows. It gives a real sense of the light of the world chasing away the darkness, of hope filling the void of despair.

I do wonder if hymns sometimes get a bad press in the church today. When I recently asked my friend Oli to suggest some manly worship songs, he replied, 'That's no problem, I'll use songs like "Beloved, I want to feel your kisses" and "Jesus, I want to be your girlfriend".' Clearly we men are concerned about the feminisation of church worship, but I'm pleased to see that we're fighting back. At Christian Vision for Men's 'The Gathering', in a field near Swindon, the mess tent was rocking to 'Tins and Hymns' as more than a thousand blokes took a pint in one hand and belted out 'Amazing Grace' for all they were worth.

Song-time has featured on and off at our Who Let The Dads Out? group over the years, and we know that it's a popular element of many groups around the country and overseas. The idea of leading a bunch of men and their children in a rendition of 'The wheels on the bus' or 'My God is a great big God' fills me with dread, but the other week I had a revelation as I visited another group near Manchester. Towards the end of their session, the dads and children were encouraged to form a big circle and do the 'Hokey cokey'. Even I could manage that! It was such a delight to see and hear dads, grandfathers and children roaring in and out together. Could this constitute praise and worship?

Dear Lord, we ask for your help as we seek to understand the meaning of praise and worship. We want the dads and children in our group to experience just a little of what it means to worship you, whether through singing a joyful song or drawing a picture that captures the beauty of your creation or simply thanking you for a breakfast butty.

April activity: Eggy Easter garden

You can't have an Easter Who Let The Dads Out? without having a bash at the classic Easter garden. The more ambitious among you might want to speak to the minister and propose that Who Let The Dads Out? take on the project of creating a substantive Easter garden to form a frontispiece in the church. In fact, in my mind's eye I can see men across the country already starting to plan a major construction project. But here we'll keep it simple.

You will need:

- Eggs (1 per dad and child)
- Bag of gravel
- Twigs (2 per dad and child)
- Thread
- Bag of moss
- Plastic plates (1 per dad and child)
- Black permanent marker pen

You can forage for gravel, twigs and moss or make a quick trip to a garden centre.

Preparation

Hard-boil the eggs beforehand or soft-boil them at the group. Build an example garden (see page 106).

The families must:

- Carefully cut the top off the egg and scoop out the contents. (Why not eat the egg with toast soldiers?)
- Put the top of the egg aside to be the rolled-away stone. Draw a black 'cave' entrance on the upturned remainder of the egg.
- Place an adequate amount of moss on the plate.
- Bind the two twigs together with thread to make a cross.
- Arrange the egg, gravel path and cross on the moss.

The craft leader must:

- Have a passion for gardening!

*

ALL ABOARD THE WHO LET THE DADS OUT? EXPRESS!

Who Let The Dads Out? sessions can often be busy and it may be difficult to get time to chat at length with the dads who come. A good way of deepening relationships and creating some very strong memories as a group is to meet up between sessions for an outing of some sort. There is no need for an outing to become all-consuming or for the arrangements to cause you palpitations and sleepless nights. Try to keep things simple. The best way we have discovered to do that is by taking a train journey.

When I asked Megan and Billy what they remembered most about the Who Let The Dads Out? trips we have been on, they said it was the train journey and paddling in the sea. Our excursions have been to Llandudno, a seaside town in North Wales, which is just over an hour away by train. We would arrange to meet at the railway station at a certain time and all buy our own tickets. No one needed to sign up in advance. If people were there in time for the train, we knew they were going, and if they were not there, we knew they were not going—very straightforward. If anyone happened to be late, they could always jump on a later train and link up with us in Llandudno.

Some families took packed lunches and some bought lunch later. Mostly, we stayed together as a group, but occasionally families would branch off on their own or in smaller groups. The one thing everyone knew was the time of the train we would catch to return home, but even then, if someone was late, they would just catch the next train.

We played football and cricket on the beach, built sandcastles, walked along the pier, ventured into the amusement arcades and got to know each other a lot better. We also caused a lot of people to stare and a few to raise their eyebrows; I can still vividly recall a conversation with some pensioners on the train who assumed that we must all be single dads as no women were present to look after the children.

For days, months and years after our outings, the dads still talk about our trips to the seaside. A forest or hill or park or town may be just as much fun if you are not near enough to the seaside. Why not give it a try?

Ten ideas for Who Let The Dads Out? outings

- Kite-flying at the park or playing field
- Visiting a castle
- A night-time walk in the dark with torches
- Feeding the ducks at the local pond, canal or river
- Den building in a forest
- An autumn walk, kicking leaves and splashing in puddles
- Teddy bear picnic in the park
- Meeting up at a soft play centre
- Conker collecting
- An animal spotting walk around the local community

*

— MAY —

ENTERTAINING ANGELS

We often describe children as little angels (generally other people's children!). This month we would like to encourage you to reflect on how you welcome unusual people to your Who Let The Dads Out? group, and then get your little angels and their fathers making their very own angels, with hair that grows.

May reflection

Keep on loving each other as brothers and sisters. Do not forget to show hospitality to strangers, for by so doing some people have shown hospitality to angels without knowing it.
HEBREWS 13:1–2

When I was growing up, a regular caller to our house was a gypsy woman. She was old and lined, dirty and dishevelled, and her speech was poor. She came to sell small posies of wild flowers and bunches of pussy willow for a few pennies each, and she was given short shrift at many of the homes in our village. People spotted her coming and would not open the door, or, if they did, they would say, 'No thank you' with strained politeness and see her on her way as quickly as possible. Few wanted to be seen associating with a woman of this sort, but, to my acute youthful embarrassment, my mother was one of the exceptions. She would not only open the door to her; she would buy whatever the old lady was selling and then fetch her a cup of water and chat to her—on the front step in full view of the neighbours—while the woman thirstily drank every last drop.

I could not understand why my mother chose to associate with someone who was shunned by many of the other decent people in our community, so one day I asked her. I will never forget my mother's reply. 'It says in the Bible that some people entertain angels without knowing it,' she said. She did not need to say anything more. I learnt an important lesson that day.

Most of the dads at your Who Let The Dads Out? group this month will be fairly familiar to you, but there may also be new people—strangers who perhaps look a bit out of place, even uncomfortable. They could be very different from the rest of the fathers; maybe they lack social skills and do not mix very well. Perhaps the families are not dressed as tidily as the others, and the dad might appear to be struggling to control his children. Possibly they make you and the other fathers feel a bit ill-at-ease. But imagine if you knew that the stranger in your midst was an angel sent by God. While I hope I treat everybody I meet with love and respect, simply because that is the right thing to do and not just because of who they might turn out to be, I have to acknowledge that if I knew the man was an angel, it would certainly affect the way I felt about him, and I would be bound to give him special attention.

The lesson I learnt the day I asked my mother why she was so kind to the poor gypsy woman was that I should treat each person I meet as if they were an angel sent by God. It is a good principle to bear in mind when we entertain strangers in our Who Let The Dads Out? groups.

Pray that God would bring strangers to your Who Let The Dads Out? group and that they all, regardless of appearance or personality, would discover a loving, warm and generous welcome among you.

Father God, please bring strangers into the midst of our Who Let The Dads Out? group, and help us to love them as brothers and entertain them as angels. Amen

May activity: Angelic grass heads

You will need:
- Sawdust
- Grass seed
- Tablespoons
- Small elastic bands
- Googly eyes
- Stickers
- Clean pairs of old tights (enough for each child to have one foot each)
- Felt-tip pens
- Angel wing templates on gold or silver card (10 cm × 15 cm) (see page 107)
- Strong glue or double-sided tape
- Modelling wire
- Sparkly tinsel
- A bottle of water to enable the children to squirt water on to their grass heads

Preparation

Cut the feet off the pairs of tights, ensuring that you have at least 20 cm lengths.

Print and cut out the angel wing templates.

The families must:

- Take one 'foot' and put a level tablespoon of grass seed into it.
- Spoon sawdust into the foot, packing it tightly. The foot needs to feel solid, and it should be about as wide and long as a large mug. Try to make sure that the grass seed remains as a layer at the toes of the foot and does not become too mixed in with the sawdust.
- Secure the open end of the foot by twisting it and tying it in a knot or putting a tight elastic band around it.
- Bang the knotted end on the table to flatten the base so that it will stand up on its own.
- From the centre of the ball, pinch out some of the nylon and sawdust, and twist it to form a nose. Secure the nose with a tight elastic band.
- Stick googly eyes above the nose and draw on a smiling mouth.
- Use strong glue or double-sided tape to attach the angel wings to the back of the head.
- Make a halo by twisting the wire into a circle with a long stem and poking it into the top of the head.
- Decorate the halo with sparkly tinsel.
- Water the grass seed.

The craft leader must:

- Remind the families to water their grass heads regularly and liberally.

*

— JUNE —

I LOVE YOU, DAD

We are marking Father's Day by thinking about the relationship that Noah had with his sons and what it can teach us about the importance of trust between fathers and their children. We stick with the Noah theme by offering an idea for a rainbow Father's Day gift.

June reflection

Noah was a righteous man, blameless among the people of his time, and he walked faithfully with God. Noah had three sons: Shem, Ham and Japheth.
GENESIS 6:9–10

On that very day Noah and his sons, Shem, Ham and Japheth, together with his wife and the wives of his three sons, entered the ark.
GENESIS 7:13

This month we celebrate Father's Day, an opportunity to remember, acknowledge and thank our fathers and father figures for what they have done for us. Who Let The Dads Out?, by its nature, celebrates fathers every session, but this month presents an opportunity to make a special effort to honour the fathers and father figures in our groups.

Of course, not all fathers are good fathers, and even the best can be exasperating at times. Imagine how Shem, Ham and Japheth would have felt about their father Noah when he claimed that he had heard from God and, as a result, would be building an ark and filling it with animals. I think that if I had been Noah's son, I would have been a touch embarrassed, to say the least. The ridicule that you would endure if your father was the neighbourhood nutter building a big boat in the front yard and, at the first sign of rain, shepherding you, your wife and a vast collection of animals on board, would be unbearable. Even the best father would struggle to retain credibility in the eyes of his children if that happened. At some point, though, Shem, Ham and Japheth chose to trust their father, despite his crazy ideas, and their faith was rewarded. The ark sailed and their lives were saved. Their father had protected them, just as Noah's Father God had protected him. It is a fantastic and inspiring story of the special trust between fathers and children.

At their age, most of the children in your Who Let The Dads Out? group will trust their fathers naturally and implicitly, and will rely on them for protection. If any of their dads announced that they would be building a boat in the garden and would set sail when it began to rain, the children would be thrilled! But as children get older and realise that their dads are only human, trust can be more difficult to maintain and relationships can even turn sour. The fathers and children in your group need prayer, not just for their relationships now but for the way they will be in the future.

If you get the chance at your Who Let The Dads Out? session, ask some of the dads about their hopes for the future. Questions such as 'Do you like where you live?', 'Do you think you will stay in your job for ever?' and 'Where will your child go to school?' can prompt a dad to open up about his thoughts and plans for what life may hold for him and his family, and will allow you to pray for them with more insight. Perhaps you will even feel able to tell them that you are praying for them.

Thank God for the trust between the fathers and children in your Who Let The Dads Out? group, and ask for God's protection over the families now and in the future. Pray that the fathers will choose to trust God for their protection.

Father God, thank you that Noah trusted you, his children trusted him and you protected them all. Thank you that this month we can use the opportunity of Father's Day to celebrate the trust between the fathers and children at our Who Let The Dads Out? group. Please enable us to learn more about the families who are at the session, so that we are better able to pray for them and care for them. Our greatest desire is to see the fathers and children learning to trust you more. Amen

June activity: Father's Day rainbow mosaic

You will need:

- Rainbow template on A4 card/paper (see page 108)
- Pots of different-coloured, pre-cut 1 cm squares of card or paper
- 'Happy Father's Day' crock of gold template (see page 109)
- Chocolate coins in gold foil
- Glue sticks
- Double hole punch
- Strips of ribbon, approximately 25 cm in length

Preparation

Photocopy the rainbow template, ensuring that there are enough copies for all the families.

Cut out the 1 cm squares of coloured card or paper.

Photocopy the 'Happy Father's Day' crock of gold template, ensuring there are enough copies for all the families.

The families must:

- Take a rainbow template.
- Glue the coloured squares, one at a time, on to the arcs of the rainbow, until the whole rainbow is full of a stunning mosaic pattern.
- Glue around the edge of the 'Happy Father's Day' crock of gold template and fix it to one end of the rainbow, so that it forms a pocket into which a gold coin can be slipped.

- Punch two holes at the top of the card above the rainbow.
- Thread a strip of ribbon through the holes and tie it on to allow the rainbow to be hung up.
- Slip a gold coin into the 'Happy Father's Day' crock at the end of the rainbow.

The craft leader must:

- Encourage the children who are old enough to hide their Father's Day rainbow mosaics and give them to their fathers/male carers on Father's Day.
- If confident enough to do so, lead the families in a chorus of the Rainbow Song ('Red and yellow and pink and green...') at some point during the session.

- [illegible]
- [illegible]

The craft leader must:

- [illegible]
- [illegible]

*

THE BACON BUTTY: HOW DO YOU MAKE YOURS?

Let's be honest, the only butty to rival the bacon butty is a chip one, but chip butties don't work too well on Saturday mornings, so the signature food for Who Let The Dads Out? has become the simple construction of bacon encased in bread. The word 'butty' (which is just a slang term for a sandwich) and the consequent alliteration when it is coupled with the sandwich content, bacon, has helped it gain its iconic status. However, there are other factors that come into play, especially in the Who Let The Dads Out? world.

The bacon butty has man appeal. Why there is something masculine about a simple sandwich is difficult to define, but it could be to do with the hot meat contrasting with the cold bread, the opportunity to make it your own by adding your favourite sauce and the fact that you can easily eat it standing up without the niceties of cutlery and crockery. It is definitely an 'on the go' food.

The bacon butty also seems perfectly suited to a Saturday morning. After a busy working week, starting the weekend with a simple culinary treat, which you would never contemplate having on a weekday morning, is a pleasure to look forward to. It marks out Saturday as being a different sort of day—a day to relax and enjoy the good things of life. The bacon butty almost feels like a reward for getting through another week.

The bacon butty tastes great too, and that is its most

important characteristic, because if it was not so mouth-wateringly delicious, everything else about it would pale into insignificance.

We have discovered that as well as bestowing considerable benefits on its consumers, the bacon butty can be used to invest in others in the community. Some Who Let The Dads Out? groups have taken the opportunity to source their bacon and bread from local small businesses. The resulting bacon butties are second to none and have often been described as the 'best bacon butty I have ever tasted'. Group leaders have explained to their local store owners what they are doing at Who Let The Dads Out?, which has elicited wider community support. Word of mouth is a powerful advocate, and getting the local butcher or baker on your side may well result in dads and children out shopping on a Saturday morning getting tipped off about the place to get the perfect bacon butty. This means that others within your community are willingly getting involved in your outreach and evangelism, which cannot be a bad thing.

So how do you make yours? And could you do it a little differently? It may cost a bit more in financial terms, but the investment may be worthwhile in advancing the kingdom of God.

Who would have thought the humble bacon butty could have such a profound impact?

(We recognise that some groups feature alternatives to bacon butties as part of their Who Let The Dads Out? sessions. Hopefully, the principles of sourcing ingredients from businesses in the local community can still apply, whatever refreshments are provided.)

*

— JULY —

SIT DOWN NEXT TO ME

Our theme this month is 'sitting down', and, as well as looking at what can happen when we sit down with someone, our craft idea represents a perfect thing for children to sit on—a picnic blanket.

July reflection

Now he had to go through Samaria. So he came to a town in Samaria called Sychar, near the plot of ground Jacob had given to his son Joseph. Jacob's well was there, and Jesus, tired as he was from the journey, sat down by the well.

JOHN 4:4–6

It is a typical Who Let The Dads Out? session and you are busy putting out toys, making refreshments, welcoming people, clearing up and washing empty cups, overseeing the craft activity, mopping up the flood in the toilets, emptying the nappy bin and generally rushing here, there and everywhere. Before you know it, everyone has gone home with smiles on their faces and another great morning has passed. You tidy up the kitchen, put the toys away, lock up, and finally, when you reach home, you can take the weight off your feet and sit down. It is a wonderful moment! I know how difficult it will be to put into practice, but I would like to encourage you to sit down a little earlier in the morning.

In John 4 there is an account of Jesus talking with a Samaritan woman as she draws water at a well. Jesus was on a journey from Judea to Galilee and was tired, so he stopped for a break at a well and, naturally, sat down. A Samaritan woman came to the well and, despite the fact that association between a Jew and a Samaritan was culturally unacceptable, they got into a conversation. Jesus then disclosed to her that he was the Messiah she was expecting. It is an incredibly deep and momentous exchange and one which, I believe, may have been encouraged by the fact that Jesus was sitting down.

There is something about the position of sitting, rather than the more formal posture of standing, that seems to give us the security to share more openly. Sitting communicates to others that we have time to give them; it says that we are not in a rush to get away. It shows that we are relaxed, so others around us relax too. Consequently, conversation flows and relationships deepen.

I know it will be a challenge, but at your Who Let The Dads Out? session this month, please do try to sit down—even if only for five minutes—next to one of the dads, begin a conversation and let the Holy Spirit lead where it goes. The content of your exchange might seem trivial to you or it could be deep and meaningful. Whichever it is, I am sure that in the context of an expression of God's love, sitting down will be a very significant thing to do.

Ask God to guide you as you choose who to sit down with at your Who Let The Dads Out? session, and to bless whatever conversation follows.

Father God, thank you for Jesus' example to us of how to communicate with the people we encounter. At our Who Let The Dads Out? session, please give us opportunities to sit down with the dads who need us most. Amen

July activity: Picnic blankets

You will need:

- Paper strips in a variety of colours, 1.5 cm x 20 cm
- A sheet of A4 card for each child
- Coloured pencils or crayons
- Glue sticks
- A few real picnic blankets

Preparation

Cut the paper card into strips of about 1.5 cm x 20 cm.

The families must:

- Place the A4 card in a landscape position (that is, with the long sides at top and bottom).
- Choose six strips of paper in different colours and apply glue to a 1 cm section at the end of each strip.
- Fix the strips of paper, one below the other, down the left-hand side of the A4 card, about 2 cm in from the edge. Allow the glue to dry.
- Choose eight more strips of paper in a variety of colours.

- Weave one of the strips vertically through the horizontal strips that are already glued on to the card, starting under the first horizontal strip—under, over, under, over and so on.
- Weave the next strip alongside, but this time starting over the top of the first horizontal strip—over, under, over, under and so on.
- Keep weaving the strips, alternating the way they start—over or under—until the A4 card is full.
- Trim off the edges of the paper strips, leaving a 2 cm border.
- Lift up the woven 'blanket', spread glue on the A4 card and fix the blanket to the card.
- Draw the faces of the people you would like to take on a picnic, around the border.

The craft leader must:

- Spread a few real picnic blankets on the floor and encourage the families to play at having a picnic with their bacon/ breakfast butties.

*

A TALE OF TWO SETTEES

My mother and father call it a settee. Some of our friends call theirs a sofa. In our house we call it a couch. What do you call that cosy piece of furniture that is designed to seat two or more people, but is so much more comfortable when you get the whole thing to yourself?

The right couch may be the pinnacle of comfort, but it can also be the ultimate in sociability. I can still remember particular times when we have had friends over and all crammed on to the couch together to watch something on television—generally a football match or a singing competition. The atmosphere gets pretty raucous and there is a lot of pushing and shoving to gain a bit of space, but it is great fun nonetheless—and it is the being together on the couch I remember, not what we were watching. Friends of ours, the Lloyd family, have two couches in their front room. There are four people in the Lloyd family, all over the age of 15, but they prefer to squeeze up together on just one of their couches, and during the evenings the newer one remains vacant while the old, threadbare one is positively crowded.

Who Let The Dads Out? groups have discovered the power of soft furniture, as the tale of two settees at the L19: Who Let The Dads Out? at St Mary's Grassendale, in Liverpool, perfectly illustrates. At the hatch where the bacon butties are served, they leave a collection bowl for donations towards the cost of the session. They suggest an 'eat as much as you want' amount, but they leave it to the punters to decide if and what to give. The dads are always very generous and, when they discovered that they had built up quite a considerable amount of cash, the group leader, Jane Leadbetter, asked the men what they would like to spend it on. The response was unanimous: they wanted a couch! Jane presented the idea to the parochial church council and, when they sanctioned the idea, Jane asked the fathers what type they would like. 'We're not bothered,' was the response. 'We just want a couch!'

Jane discovered that the money they had saved stretched to two rather suave black leather couches—perhaps the ultimate furniture item for some men, but rarely permitted in a family home. They have positioned the couches facing each other, with a table at the side, piled high with leaflets, flyers and newspapers. Another of the group leaders, Jane's husband Ian, has found that the men don't just sit quietly on the couches reading: 'they chat about the articles they are reading in the newspapers'.

So the 'couch corner' has become a hotbed of debate about political issues and world news, but it has also had a much more profound impact, as Jane explains: 'The children relax alongside their dads on the sofas and sit on the floor using the sofas as tables. The sofas quickly become covered in crumbs and sticky patches, and you find Lego down the sides of the cushions.' In a beautiful statement, Jane perfectly sums up why a couch is so appealing to both children and dads: 'It's a little piece of home for them.'

*

— AUGUST —

TO SOAR ON WINGS LIKE EAGLES

We've got two themes for the price of one this month—running and flying! And as it's high summer (at least here in the UK), there may be the opportunity to take this theme outside.

August reflection

Do you not know?
Have you not heard?
The Lord is the everlasting God,
the Creator of the ends of the earth.
He will not grow tired or weary,
and his understanding no one can fathom.
He gives strength to the weary
and increases the power of the weak.
Even youths grow tired and weary,
and young men stumble and fall;
but those who hope in the Lord
will renew their strength.
They will soar on wings like eagles;
they will run and not grow weary,
they will walk and not be faint.
ISAIAH 40:28–31

I've always had a fondness for the book of Isaiah. Maybe it's because one of the first jokes I remember hearing as a young boy is this:

'I say, I say, I say, my dog's called Isaiah.'

'Really, why's your dog called Isaiah?'

'Because one eye's 'igher than the other!'

At a recent conference, we were taught a new worship song about running towards a goal, and consequently I found myself thinking about the idea of running in general. It's hardly surprising that this is on my mind as I've recently been training for and then participating in the Chester half-marathon (part of my '50 things to do as I'm turning 50').

The training was something of a grind. Although I've always loved running around in pursuit of a ball, the idea of running in straight lines has never fired my imagination, and having failed to put in as many miles of training as I'd wanted, I knew that the last few miles of the Chester half-marathon were going to be a real slog.

By contrast, children are amazing. They just love to run around. At our sessions with older children (aged four to seven), we have to drag them away from the footie or the Uni-hoc and send them red-faced through to the hatch to get a drink of squash. Of course, children also have their limits, and sometimes they seem to go from boundless energy to collapsing with exhaustion at the flick of a switch. I love that moment in *The Incredibles* when, just after they've saved the world, Dash is saying to his dad, 'That was the best vacation ever…' and promptly falls fast asleep on the back seat of the car.

That's also why I love this passage from Isaiah. It's rooted in an everyday truth but is hugely inspirational at the same time. It reminds us that our Father is the God of the impossible. It applies to me and you when we're running a Who Let The Dads Out? group or any other ministry. It applies in our working lives, and our home lives. It applies on all our front-lines. I encourage you to ask God to give you strength and increase your power this week.

What of my half-marathon exploits? I certainly prayed on the start line at the Chester half-marathon that I would run and not grow weary, walk and not be faint—and even that I might soar on wings like eagles. Well, I didn't quite soar, but I did manage a respectable time and exceeded my expectations. I think my prayers were answered.

Dear Lord, we do know and we have heard that you are the everlasting God, who does not grow tired or weary, but we also forget. In fact, we forget really quickly. We walk out of church on a Sunday morning, get confronted by the challenges of this world, and our hope in you tends to shrink. Then we stumble and fall.

For our sakes, and for the sake of the kingdom, we pray that you would be like a patient father with us, Lord. Build our faith so that we might renew our strength. Build it through our times of prayer and Bible study, through corporate worship, through the stories we share with our Christian friends and family and, above all, by touching our lives in godly ways that we cannot deny. Amen

August activity: Kite collage

You will need:

- A4 coloured paper for the background (suggested colours: blue, green or purple), one sheet per person
- Coloured paper for the kite (suggested colours: yellow and red), cut into small triangles, four per person (see illustration on page 110)
- Cotton wool balls
- String or wool
- Dried pasta bows
- PVA glue
- Scissors

Preparation

So that the dads and children can concentrate on creating their kite picture, you can prepare by cutting out four kite triangles for each person.

The families must:

- Take one background A4 sheet and apply four dabs of PVA glue where they want the kite to go.
- Arrange the four kite triangle pieces and stick them on the background sheet.
- Cut a piece of string or wool to form the tail, and get sticky by putting some glue on it and arranging it in a curve on the picture.

- Take about six pasta bows, add dabs of glue and stick the bows on the tail of the kite.
- Take some cotton wool, add dabs of glue and stick the cotton wool on the background of the picture to form clouds.

The craft leader must:

- If confident to do so, lead a chorus of 'Let's go fly a kite' from *Mary Poppins*. Alternatively, get hold of the soundtrack and play the song in the background while the activity is taking place.

*

— SEPTEMBER —

AS FOR ME AND MY HOUSEHOLD

As we start a new term, our theme is based on the stories of Joshua. Joshua's story is intrinsically linked to God's plan for the people of Israel to enter the promised land. We are reminded of how he captured the city of Jericho and also his final words to his people: 'Choose this day whom you will serve.'

September reflection

'Now fear the Lord and serve him with all faithfulness. Throw away the gods your ancestors worshipped beyond the River Euphrates and in Egypt, and serve the Lord. But if serving the Lord seems undesirable to you, then choose for yourselves this day whom you will serve, whether the gods your ancestors served beyond the Euphrates, or the gods of the Amorites, in whose land you are living. But as for me and my household, we will serve the Lord.'
JOSHUA 24:14–15

The book of Joshua tells the story of the Israelites' entry into the land that God had promised them, and of how they conquered the land, divided it among the tribes and settled down to live there after years of nomadic existence, hardship and war. Of course, as a child, my knowledge of Joshua was dominated by the story of how he led his people to victory in the battle of Jericho, and of the remarkable faith of a man who was happy to make his army march round and round the city in what must have seemed a futile exercise.

When I read about Joshua now, it's hard to look beyond the complex legacy that exists in the Middle East today as various nations and peoples struggle to maintain their identity in a hostile atmosphere. The human condition seems to dictate that we crave peace but are destined to struggle all our lives.

Joshua 23 starts with the words 'After a long time had passed and the Lord had given Israel rest from all their enemies around them...' This reminds me that God doesn't promise us an easy life. There will be struggles aplenty, as there were for Joshua, but God does offer us times of rest. This is both a promise and a challenge. It means that we are challenged to look out for others who may need rest, and do what we can to help them get it—whether by playing our part at home, cooking a meal for a couple who have just become parents, or making a donation to support a young carers' charity.

I'm also aware that times of rest can be dangerous times. When we are striving and struggling to achieve something, we are focused and driven. Once we achieve our short-term goal, kick back and relax, how often do we pick up a bug, lose our fitness or find our minds wandering in dangerous ways?

The words in Joshua 24:14–15 are part of Joshua's final speech to the leaders of Israel before he dies at the ripe old age of 110. There is definitely a sense in which he is the nation's father-figure, seeking to pass on the wisdom that he has gained and to encourage his 'children' to walk in the way of the Lord. He knows that the challenge has only just begun, that conquering Canaan is only like establishing base camp before setting out to climb Everest—and, of course, history proves him right.

But what words he offers those that will follow on! They are a warning, a challenge and a rallying call all rolled up in the cry 'As for me and my household, we will serve the Lord.' The idea of the father as the head of the household may be less fashionable these days, but there's still plenty of statistical evidence to suggest that men who put their faith in God will ultimately be part of a whole Christian household. Maybe there's a dad at your Who Let The Dads Out? group who is just starting the journey towards Christian faith. Perhaps it will be a long and winding road that he needs to travel, guided by someone within the group who is able to become his close friend. Maybe, by God's grace, his faith will grow, and his positive parental influence on his children and in his home will grow into a determination to serve the Lord. 'As for me and my household...'

Abba, Father, sometimes you ask us to do things that seem strange to us. Just as Joshua must have stepped outside his comfort zone as he sought to conquer Jericho, so you sometimes ask us to take a chance, but we are also reminded that you keep your promises. Joshua was victorious. We too want to be victorious for you. We want to speak blessings over the dads and children in our Who Let The Dads Out? group and to see their hearts turned towards you. Help us, we pray. Amen

September activity: Jericho toast

You will need:

- Thick sliced white bread
- A toaster
- A choice of spreads (for example, soft cheese spread, peanut butter, jam)
- A packet of ridged crisps (such as Frazzles) to make the walls of Jericho
- A packet of jelly babies to make the army marching around the walls

Preparation

No preparation is required. See example on page 111.

The families must:

- Take a slice of toast each, and add their spread of choice.
- Take five pieces of 'wall'.
- Take three jelly babies.
- Push the wall pieces into the toast so that they stand up.
- Stick the jelly babies on to the spread.
- Pose for pictures.
- Cause the walls to come tumbling down by eating their completed snack.
- Go home and recreate the activity again and again.

The craft leader must:

- Subject to parental consent, take pictures of the group's Jericho toast creations to post on the Who Let The Dads Out? Facebook group page.

*

TOP TEN TV AND MOVIE VEHICLES

This top ten list is for the ten 'best' vehicles from TV and the movies, counting down to number one.

You can create your own list in advance and compare lists towards the end of the session. Alternatively, you can use our list:

1. The Batmobile
2. The Millennium Falcon from *Star Wars*
3. The Death Star from *Star Wars*
4. The three Mini Coopers from *The Italian Job*
5. Thunderbird 2 (and Thunderbird 4, because it came inside Thunderbird 2)
6. Aston Martin DB5 from *Goldfinger* and *Skyfall*
7. De Lorean from *Back to the Future*
8. The Tardis
9. USS Enterprise
10. Del Boy's Reliant Robin from *Only Fools and Horses*

*

— OCTOBER —

GHOSTBUSTERS

Here in the UK the nights are closing in. Winter is coming. At the end of the month, children will be knocking on our doors dressed as skeletons and vampires, demanding sweets with 'menaces'. So this month we're going to think about what makes us scared and, more importantly, how our faith helps us conquer our fear.

October reflection

For you did not receive a spirit that makes you a slave again to fear, but you received the Spirit of sonship. And by him we cry, 'Abba, Father.'
ROMANS 8:15 (NIV 1984)

When my daughter Laura was younger, my wife and I had to think hard about what attitude we should take regarding Halloween. It wasn't difficult generally to discourage the idea of her going trick or treating, although there was one year when one of her best friends had a Halloween-themed party and we had to decide whether we should let her dress up and go or not. These are not easy decisions for parents, and I'm very supportive of churches that put on 'light parties' as an alternative. Our theme for next month is light, so I'm looking forward to having the light shine in the darkness. But for now it's getting dark, and I'm getting a bit scared…

Being scared is an interesting thing, isn't it? It's such a raw emotion. When we are young, we need those who love us and know what's best for us to help us learn not to be scared. Once we're older, though, we seem to crave the experience of fear. Many of us say we love to be scared. Ghost stories have been around for years. Since the early days of cinema, we've chosen to watch horror films. Adrenalin junkies will chase the next extreme nerve-shredding and death-cheating experience. People say, 'When I'm scared, I know that I'm alive.'

When I was a student in Coventry, I shared a rented house that was supposed to be haunted. Certainly at that time I would have felt sure that ghosts don't exist, as the concept of spirits of the dead being trapped on earth was inconsistent with my understanding of what the Bible says happens when we die. But that didn't stop me being scared almost witless by incidents that ultimately could be explained, but which, at the time, filled me with fear—like the time when I was alone in the house one weekend and suddenly the television died and all the lights went out. Having frantically groped my way to the front door in the pitch dark, I was able to establish that the whole street was in darkness because of a power cut. Then there was the time when my housemates had gone to the pub and I'd said I would catch them up as soon as I'd finished my bath. (I should explain that this house was a typical two-up, two-down terrace, with the bathroom beyond the kitchen on the ground floor.) Wrapped only in a towel, I walked out of the bathroom and through the kitchen, and my entry into the lounge just happened to coincide with my friends (who had come back because of a change of plan) saying 'Hi'. This simple act caused me to jump out of my skin and literally over the sofa. Fortunately I didn't jump out of the towel, although I suspect it must have flown up around my waist in the process. Not a pretty sight!

I guess we've all experienced moments of extreme fear, especially when we were younger and more easily frightened. We need to learn to face and overcome our fears, and this is where our parents can help us, reassuring us through our first inoculations, visits to the hairdresser, learning to swim, and so on. Father-figures also have a role to play in our learning to overcome the things that scare us. Maybe our Who Let The Dads Out? groups can help on this journey for the children who come with their dads.

Romans 8:15 does not promise that we won't ever be scared, but it does promise that we need not become a 'slave again to fear'. Before we become Christians, we can indeed be enslaved by fear, particularly the fear of living our lives with a continuous restlessness and sense of searching, and, of course, a fear of death. Christian faith offers us freedom from that fear, a freedom embedded in the spirit of sonship—a sense of being home, safe, in the bosom of our family. We are where we belong, with our Dad and out of danger, for eternity. That spirit of sonship has been purchased for us by Jesus and given freely to us as a precious gift, by our loving Father.

Dear Lord, we thank you that we are your sons and daughters, accepted into your family. Thank you that we need not be enslaved to fear, because you have adopted us. Thank you that you have given us a hope for the future, both throughout our earthly lives and also beyond death, so that we need not fear death as the end of our being. Help us to live in the reality of this hope. Amen

October activity: 'Fear not' bracelet

You will need:
- A pack of wooden letter beads
- A pack of coloured wooden beads
- Thread or string
- Scissors

Beads are widely available online or from craft shops. They are typically 9 mm square with a 3 mm threading hole. Suitable threads are also available, or you can use ordinary string.

Preparation

Make an example to show. Pre-cut lengths of thread or string, of about 24 cm: they need to be long enough to go round a child's wrist and be tied in place. Excess string can always be trimmed after the bracelet has been tied.

The families must:

- Sort out the necessary letter beads to make a short message. The suggested words for this activity are 'Fear not', although, if the craft is popular, you could use it regularly and create relevant other messages.
- Choose some unlettered coloured beads to add to the bracelet.
- Thread the beads on the string.
- Tie the completed bracelets on to the children's wrists.

The craft leader must:

- Be able to spell!

*

THE LONG VIEW: LIFE AFTER WHO LET THE DADS OUT?

With his children, Mollie and Phoebe, now twelve and nine years old respectively, it is some time since Alan Kift has been to Who Let The Dads Out? But for a substantial period of his daughters' early lives, he was very involved in all of the activities for dads at Hoole Baptist Church in Chester.

Alan first went along to Who Let The Dads Out? when his wife Kay brought home a flyer from the weekday parent-and-toddler group that she attended. Mollie was then just a year old. After a few sessions, which he and Mollie thoroughly enjoyed, Alan noticed how the small group of volunteers struggled to tidy up at the end of the morning, so he offered to help. He would arrive early to help set out the toys and stayed until everything had been put away and the vacuuming had been done. Often that was Mollie's favourite time of the morning because the emptying hall left her with more space to run around and enjoy a game of cat-and-mouse with the vacuum cleaner—controlled by her dad!

Two years later, Mollie's sister Phoebe arrived in the Kift family and joined Who Let The Dads Out? too. By this stage, all the other dads knew that Alan was one of the group leaders, and he would particularly look out for new dads at the group to welcome them and introduce them to others.

Alan took part in a Daddy Cool! parenting programme, and the weekly dads' kickabout reactivated his footballing talents. When Mollie and Phoebe became too old for Who

Let The Dads Out?, they joined School's Out, Dad's About (SODA) Club, and Alan would try to turn it into an illicit adventure for them by saying, 'Let's go and have toast, and Mummy won't know anything about it!'

When we talk to Alan now, he has fond memories of those early years in his children's lives and of the opportunities that Who Let The Dads Out? gave to him and his family.

When I recall Who Let The Dads Out?, all I think about is the bacon butties! No, seriously, my strongest memory is of meeting and talking to like-minded dads. I'm not the most confident person, but Who Let The Dads Out? forced us together and I made new friends. I played football with them, which I had not done for 20 years.

I think Mollie and Phoebe loved spending time with me on their own. It was quality time, and they got to see me helping out. I wanted to show the girls how to help, which is why I became a governor of their school. My volunteering at Who Let The Dads Out? was a great opportunity to role-model how to help others. Daddy Cool! was useful, too. It helped me to appreciate the benefit in taking time out from difficult parenting situations and thinking them through before acting. I'm never going to get it right all the time, but I have to do my best.

Alan believes in God, and he is grateful for the activities the church runs, but he does not want to go to church every week.

I think it's good that churches do these types of things. It's a way of the church engaging with the community and overcoming the stigma that only old people are involved with church. It shows that the church is warm to people and makes them feel welcome.

If people are questioning, it may draw them to church more. Although I don't want to go to church on a Sunday, I've embraced all these activities and we do go to the services the school holds at church. We explain to the girls what is being done so that they can understand and make their own choices.

Five years on, Alan still misses Who Let The Dads Out?

Although I spend lots of time with Mollie and Phoebe, I miss meeting up with other men and having a chat. I don't get that any more, but it was great while it lasted. Who Let The Dads Out? is a winner because it brings dads and kids together.

We miss Alan, Mollie and Phoebe, too.

*

— NOVEMBER —

LIGHT FANTASTIC

The theme of our reflection and craft is a perfect antidote to the darkness of November. It is all about creating light.

November reflection

'You are the light of the world. A town built on a hill cannot be hidden. Neither do people light a lamp and put it under a bowl. Instead they put it on its stand, and it gives light to everyone in the house. In the same way, let your light shine before others, that they may see your good deeds and glorify your Father in heaven.'
MATTHEW 5:14–16

After a week of hard work, evening meetings and household commitments, the thing I look forward to most is a leisurely Saturday morning cup of tea in bed while reading the morning newspaper. Sometimes, as silly as it may sound, that thought can be the only thing that gets me through the week; to use a well-known metaphor, I feel I am travelling through a tunnel, with the light at the end becoming brighter as I approach it. I know it is only a cup of tea and an extra hour in bed, but it really does mean that much to me.

I must acknowledge, though, that I rely on others to provide me with this weekly shot of 'light'—the newsagent, the newspaper delivery boy, the workers at the power station who are busy generating electricity for my kettle and, when I am lucky, my wife, Su, who gets up to make the tea.

When I was leading our church's Who Let The Dads Out? group, often the last thing I felt like doing at the start of a weekend was getting up early, opening the church building, setting out toys, grilling bacon and making endless cups of coffee for other people. Even if they were only once a month, Who Let The Dads Out? sessions came around surprisingly quickly. However, by the end of every session, without fail, I was excited and energised in my spirit by what had happened during the morning, because I could see what impact it was having on the fathers and their children and how much they valued and appreciated this period of bright light at the beginning of a weekend. Some even described it as the highlight of the week.

As a Who Let The Dads Out? leader, you are enriching other people's lives by providing this much-needed light for them. Thank God for the privilege of being a light-giver and pray that the families at your Who Let The Dads Out? group will 'see your good deeds and glorify your Father in heaven'.

Father God, thank you for the opportunity to let the light of our faith shine before others. Please may the fathers and children at our Who Let The Dads Out? group see that what we do for them is because of our love for you. Amen

November activity: Magic torches

You will need:

- A plastic torch for each child (available relatively cheaply at discount stores, pound shops, and so on), if possible, with a lens that can be unscrewed.
- A selection of hole punches that produce holes in different shapes—for example, stars, hearts, rabbits, teddy bears (available from craft stores and online craft providers). Make sure the shape is small enough to fit within the diameter of the torch lens.
- Thin card cut into circles the same size as the torch lens.
- Crêpe paper, tissue paper or tinsel, shredded into streamers about 20–30 cm long.
- Sticky tape.
- Stickers of stars or other small designs.
- Batteries—lots of them.

Preparation

Cut out the circles of card (enough to provide one for each torch and some spares).

Shred the crêpe paper, tissue paper or tinsel into 20–30 cm streamers.

The families must:

- Choose which shape they would like for their beam of light and use the appropriate hole punch to make that shape of hole in one of the circles of card.
- Using sticky tape, attach the streamers around the bottom of the torch handle, so that they trail when the child holds the torch.
- Decorate the barrel of the torch with the stickers.
- Unscrew the lens of the torch and place the circle of card, with the shape cut out, on the outside of the lens (it must be on the outside, otherwise the bulb may scorch the card) and reassemble the torch.
- Insert the batteries.
- Switch the torch on and project the shape on to the wall or ceiling.

The craft leader must:

- At some point in the session, create a darkened room by switching off the lights and closing the curtains so that the families can enjoy shining their torches on to the walls and ceilings together.

*

— DECEMBER —

AWAY IN A MANGER

This month we are celebrating Joseph, the earthly father of Jesus. In a fitting way to finish the year, we are reminding ourselves of how special it is to be a father or father-figure. The craft idea focuses on the reason for Christmas—the birth of Jesus—and the Son of God's first bed in a humble manger. Happy Christmas!

December reflection

But after he had considered this, an angel of the Lord appeared to him in a dream and said, 'Joseph son of David, do not be afraid to take Mary home as your wife, because what is conceived in her is from the Holy Spirit. She will give birth to a son, and you are to give him the name Jesus, because he will save his people from their sins.'
MATTHEW 1:20–21

In our Christmas celebrations—the nativity plays, readings, sermons, songs and reflections—we often focus on God's choice of Mary to be the mother of Jesus. Mary's role and status are rightly emphasised, but we can overlook Joseph and diminish his importance. If we are not careful, we can even make him incidental to the Christmas story: he becomes a background figure.

It is good to remind ourselves that Joseph, as well as Mary, was chosen by God: he was chosen to be Jesus' earthly father. I do not believe that God would have made his decision for Mary to be the mother of Jesus without considering who the man in her life was and whether he was worthy to become the father of his Son. God knew that Joseph possessed the character and potential to make a good father, and he trusted him with the most significant position of earthly fatherhood that there will ever be. God called Joseph to be a father.

It is easy to forget that the role of father is special and privileged. It is not incidental to the story of our and our children's lives. We must work hard to avoid diminishing the importance of fatherhood and making fathers into background figures in family life. Fatherhood (not just biological fatherhood but being a father-figure, too) is a calling, and our Who Let The Dads Out? groups recognise and celebrate this fact every single month.

The December session is a good time to remember and celebrate the fact that all of the fathers, stepfathers, grandfathers, godfathers and father-figures in your Who Let The Dads Out? group have been chosen by God to play a unique and special part in the lives of their children, just as Joseph was called by God to be a father to Jesus. Why not go into this month's session with the aim of giving specific encouragement to at least one of the men there? In some way, try to let him know how valuable he is as a father. A simple question like 'Why do you come to Who Let The Dads Out?' can help to lead into such a conversation.

Thank God that the men who come to your building this month have the privilege of being called to be fathers and father-figures, mirroring God's fatherhood role here on earth.

Ask him for opportunities to tell the dads how special they are.

Father God, thank you for giving us your Son, Jesus, and thank you that you chose Joseph to become his father here on earth. Thank you that you called the men in our group to fatherhood too. Please give us the opportunities and words to communicate this truth to encourage the dads in this month's session. Amen

December activity: Manger cakes

You will need:
- Shredded wheat (allow approximately a third of one for each child)
- Cooking chocolate, suitable for melting
- Jelly babies (one per cake)
- Cake cases
- Fondant icing (in whichever colour you would like Jesus' blanket to be)
- Mixing bowl, wooden spoon, and microwave or hob
- Sandwich bags (just large enough to hold a manger cake)

Preparation

Make sure the children wash their hands.

Break up the shredded wheat into smaller pieces. Break up the fondant icing into grape-sized pieces.

The families must:

- All lightly break up their pieces of shredded wheat into one large mixing bowl, so that the wheat is like strands of straw (but not so broken that it turns to powder).
- When the craft leader has poured the melted chocolate over the shredded wheat, take it in turns to stir the mixture with the wooden spoon until the shredded wheat is coated in chocolate, being careful not to crush the wheat.
- Spoon some of the mixture into a cake case and place a jelly baby on top.
- Take a piece of fondant icing and, using fingers, squish it, squeeze it and flatten it out to make a blanket for baby Jesus.
- Place the fondant blanket over the jelly baby on top of the shredded wheat and put the manger cake to one side to dry and set.
- At the end of the session, put the manger into a sandwich bag so that it can be carried safely home.

The craft leader must:

- While the families are breaking up their pieces of shredded wheat, melt the chocolate in the microwave or on the hob (as per the instructions on the chocolate packet), making sure the chocolate does not burn.
- When the chocolate has melted, quickly pour it over the shredded wheat in the mixing bowl.

ACTIVITY TEMPLATES

February: Heart pendants

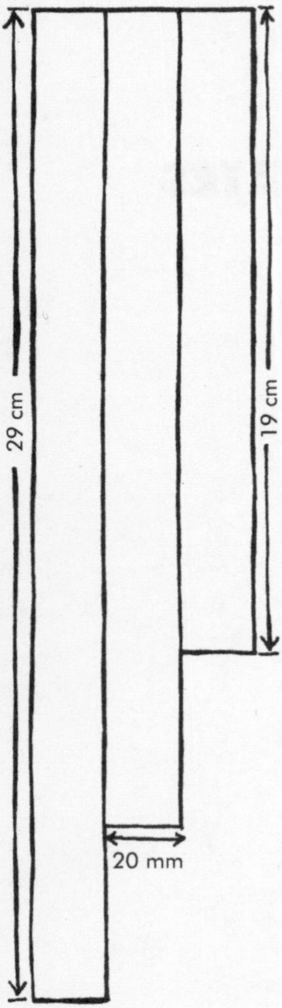

March: Cupcake gift box

Fit template to size of cupcake cases

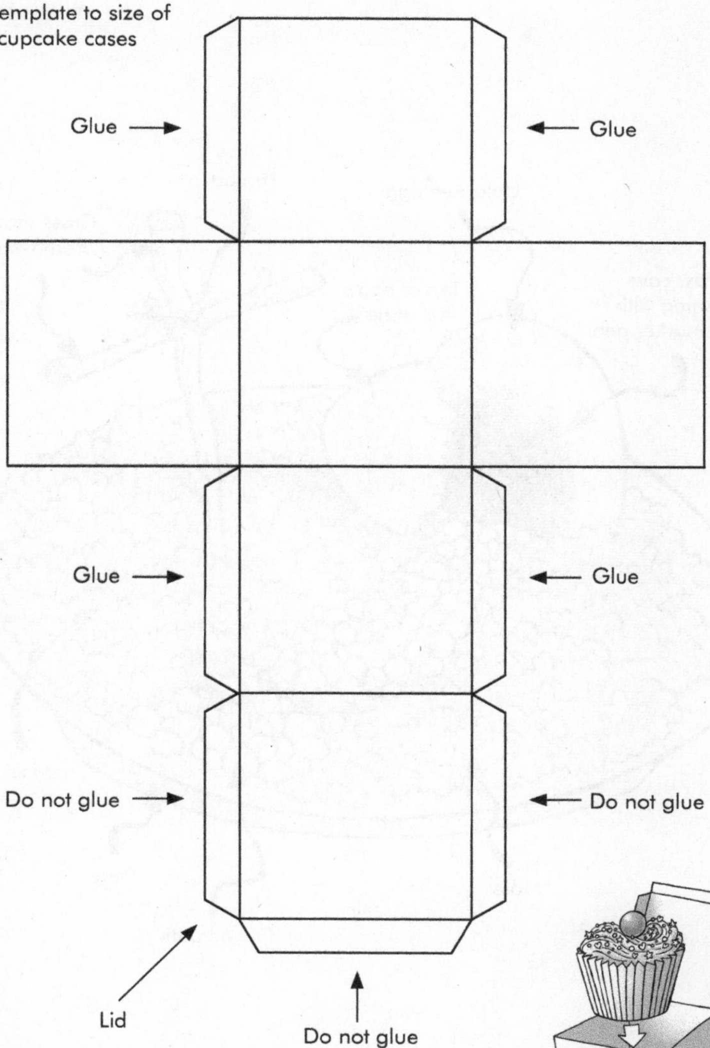

April: Easter garden

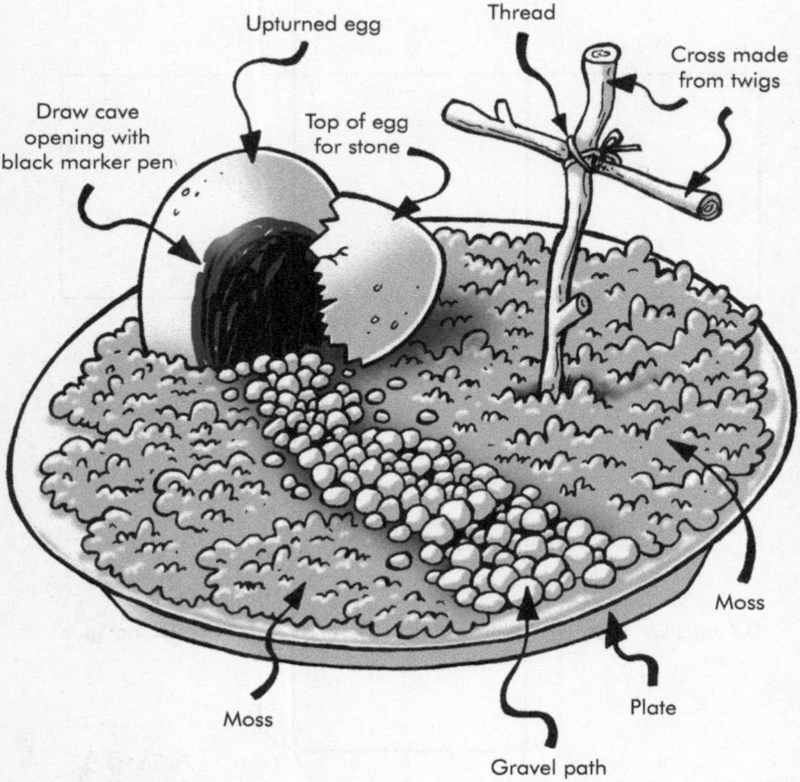

May: Angelic grass heads

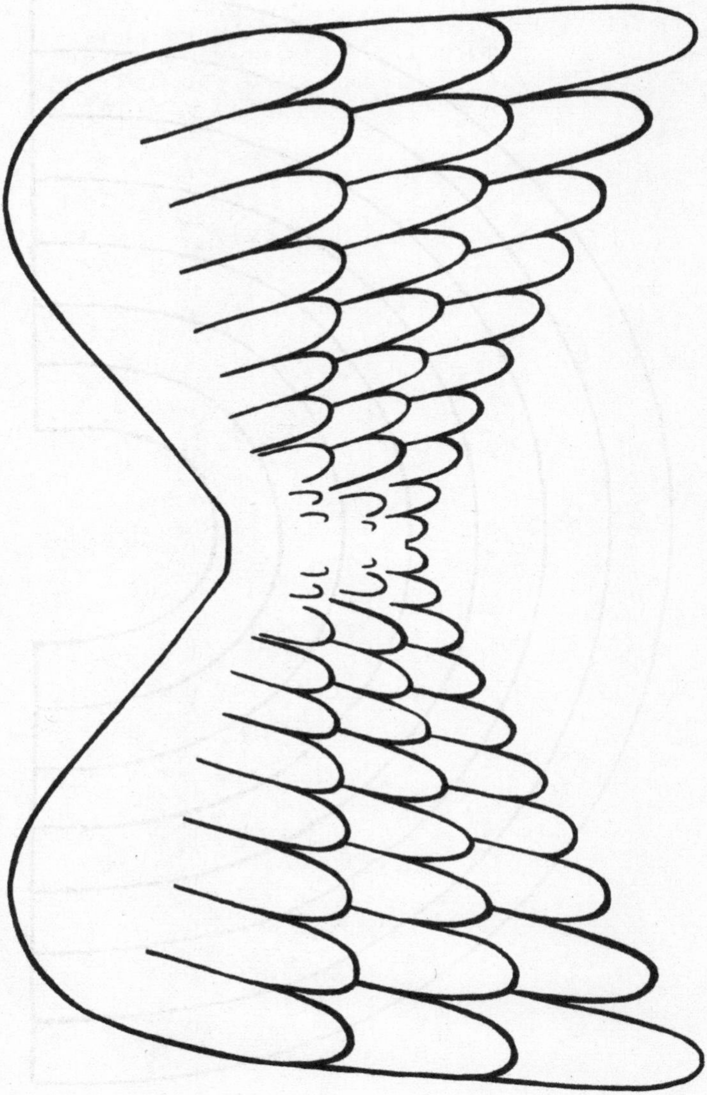

June: Rainbow mosaic

June: Crock of gold

August: Kite collage

September: Jericho toast